enj... book
... by t... ...

# Terrific TOYS

## And What They Are Made Of

By William Anthony

**BookLife**
**PUBLISHING**

©2020
**BookLife Publishing Ltd.**
**King's Lynn**
**Norfolk PE30 4LS**

All rights reserved.
Printed in Malaysia.

A catalogue record for this
book is available from the
British Library.

**ISBN:** 978-1-83927-051-2

**Written by:**
William Anthony

**Edited by:**
Madeline Tyler

**Designed by:**
Danielle Rippengill

*All facts, statistics, web addresses and URLs in this book were verified as valid and accurate at time of writing.*
*No responsibility for any changes to external websites or references can be accepted by either the author or publisher.*

## Image Credits

All images are courtesy of Shutterstock.com, unless otherwise specified. With thanks to Getty Images, Thinkstock Photo and iStockphoto. Cover – Shmelkova Nataliya, LukaKikina, Anton Mezinov, OksanaA, Just2shutter. Used on all pages – Shmelkova Nataliya. 2 – oliveromg, Yuganov Konstantin. 4 – Ulza, wavebreakmedia. 5 – anek.soowannaphoom. 6&7 – Aaron Amat. 7 – Oksana Kuzmina. 8 – NataliaL. 9 – PAKULA PIOTR. 10 – Milosz_G, wdeon. 11 – oliveromg. 12&13 – valeriiaarnaud. 13 – Rudmer Zwerver. 14 – Ulza, antoniodiaz. 15 – Yuganov Konstantin. 16 – risteski goce. 17 – TZIDO SUN. 18&19 – Yuriy Golub. 19 – AlesiaKan. 20 – Mountains Hunter. 21 – Rammy_Rammy, Robert Kneschke, zirconicusso. 22 – Edinaldo Macie, Sergey Bezgodov. 23 – cjmacer, Pressmaster.

# Contents

Words that look like this can be found in the glossary on page 24.

# Terrific Toys

Toys are the fun things that you play with. They can be made of almost anything, and they are all terrific.

What is your favourite toy?

# Material World

The things that toys are made of are called materials. Different materials can **affect** how toys feel or how they are used.

Plastic, wood and metal are some materials that are used to make toys.

# Plastic Playtime

Plastic is a material made by humans. It can be made into almost any shape or size. Lots of toys are made from it.

Plastic can be a hard material. It can sometimes be a little bit shiny, too. Building blocks, dolls and toy cars can all be made of plastic.

Plastic

# Marvellous Metal

Metal is a _natural_ material. Just like plastic, we can shape metal into lots of different shapes and sizes, such as a toy car or a scooter.

Metal

8

Metal toys can last a long time.

There are lots of different types of metal. Some metals are used for your toys because they are hard, strong and difficult to break.

# Wooden Wonders

Lots of toys, especially older toys, are made using wood. Wood is a natural material that comes from trees.

Trees are cut down for their wood.

Wood is a hard and strong material. Wooden toys last for a long time because wood is <u>durable</u>.

How many of your toys are made of wood?

Wooden house

# China and Glass

Some materials are not as durable as others. Materials such as china can break easily. Before plastic, dolls were often made using china.

China dolls can break easily, so they must be treated carefully!

12

Marbles are a type of toy made using glass. Pieces of glass are coloured and layered on top of each other to make beautiful patterns.

Some people collect marbles. Do you collect any toys?

# Paper and Cardboard

Even materials such as paper can be used to make toys! Paper aeroplanes are a fun toy that children can make themselves by folding sheets of paper in certain ways.

Ask an adult to help you make a paper aeroplane.

Cardboard is another material you can use to make your own toys. You could use an old cardboard box to make a castle or even a rocket.

What other things can you make with a cardboard box?

# Soft Play

Some toys can be soft and squishy. Teddy bears, or teddies, are a <u>popular</u> toy all over the world. Some people keep their <u>childhood</u> teddies forever!

Have you ever been on a teddy bear's picnic?

This teddy is soft and fluffy. Can you think of any other words to describe it?

Teddies and other <u>similar</u> toys are made using soft and furry materials. Cotton and felt are two types of cloth used to make soft toys.

17

# Tech Time

Today, lots of toys are electronic. Electronic toys can do lots of fun and exciting things. Electronic toys might make sounds, move about or have a screen.

Electronic toys are made from lots of different materials. They might have glass screens, metal wires covered in plastic, and much more!

# Reuse!

We can make toys out of old materials, rather than throwing the materials away. This helps to save our planet. Things that are thrown away go into landfill. Landfill is bad for our planet.

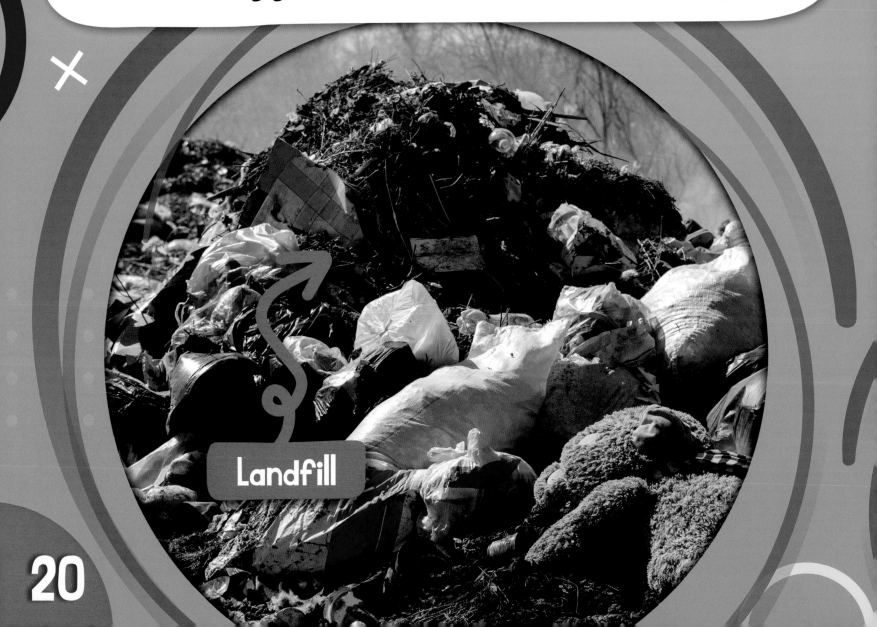

Landfill

You could make bowling pins from old plastic bottles.

You could make a toy car from old cardboard boxes.

Ask an adult for help!

You could make a telephone with two tin cans and some string.

21

# Fun Facts

The yo-yo is one of the oldest toys in the world.

The oldest type of toy in the world is thought to be the doll.

Silly Putty was taken to the Moon on the Apollo 8 space mission.

Mr Potato Head was the first toy to have a TV advert.

# Glossary

| | |
|---|---|
| advert | a message, such as a video or picture, that is used to help sell things such as toys |
| affect | cause a change in something |
| childhood | the period of time when a person is a child |
| durable | not easily broken or worn out |
| electronic | something that uses electricity to work |
| natural | found in nature and not made by people |
| popular | liked or enjoyed by many people |
| similar | almost the same as something else |

# Index